Frog and Toad Go For a Swim

Written by
Jill Atkins

Illustrated by
Mez Clark

Frog met Toad in the park.

"Let us go to the pond," said Frog.

"All right," said Toad.

"We must be quick," said Frog.
"It will soon be dark."

They set off for the pond.

Jump, jump, jump went Frog.

But she was too quick!

She fell down into a pit.

Hop, hop, hop went Toad.

He did not trip into the pit.

"Up you get, Frog," said Toad.

"You are just too quick."

Frog got up.

Then they set off for the pond.

Jump, jump, jump, went Frog.

Bump! She hit a tree.

Hop, hop, hop went Toad.

He did not hit the tree.

"Gosh!" said Toad.
"You are still too quick."

"Yes, I am," said Frog,
as she got up.

"But I will soon be at the pond."

Jump, jump, jump, went Frog.

She went down the hill to the pond.

Plop! Slish! Slosh!

Hop, hop, hop went Toad.

He went down the hill to the pond.

"You are not as quick as me," said Frog.

"But I did not end up down a pit," said Toad. "And I did not bump into a tree."

"And you did get to the pond in the end!" said Frog with a grin.

And they swam up and down the pond as the sun set.